American Art Songs
of the
Turn of the Century

EDITED BY
Paul Sperry

Dover Publications, Inc.
NEW YORK

This Dover edition, first published in 1991, is a new selection of works originally published by various American publishers, 1880–1915. (The publication information for each song appears in the table of contents.) The introduction was newly written for this edition.

We are grateful to the Free Library of Philadelphia, the Eda Kuhn Loeb Music Library of Harvard University, the Harvard Musical Association, the Library of Congress, the New York Public Library, the Bagaduce Music Lending Library and Phyllis and Neely Bruce for making a number of these song sheets available for reproduction.

We are grateful to Peer-Southern Organization for permission to reprint Charles Ives's *The Circus Band* and *Spring Song*.

Manufactured in the United States of America
Dover Publications, Inc., 31 East 2nd Street, Mineola, N.Y. 11501

Library of Congress Cataloging-in-Publication Data

American art songs of the turn of the century / edited by Paul Sperry. — 1st Dover ed.
    1 score.
    ISBN 0-486-26749-0
    1. Songs with piano. 2. Songs, English—United States. I. Sperry, Paul.
M1619.A495 1991   91-3770
                                                    CIP
                                                        M

Contents

꠸

Introduction

꾸

DESPITE THE TITLE OF this collection, it is important to remember that at the turn of the century there was no great difference between "art songs" and popular songs. In those days before recordings, songs were written to be performed mostly in homes—hence the designation "parlor songs," which we hear so often and which applies to both categories. Some were written specifically for the concert hall as others were written for the theater, but if they didn't catch on in the home they were not successful.

In this volume I have tried to include a wide variety of the "classical" styles of the day, from the lovely sentimentality of Ethelbert Nevin to the forward-looking harmonies of Louis Campbell-Tipton and Henry F. Gilbert, from the operatic style of Amy Beach to the vaudeville flavor of Sousa. The texts range in quality from the Shakespeare lyrics set by many composers to the appalling drivel of Arlo Bates's "The Danza," which now just strikes us as funny.

The majority of these composers fall within, or under the influence of, the school known as the New England Classicists, even though today we would call them romantics. Chadwick, Foote, Parker, Beach and MacDowell were the leaders of the group, Paine was their precursor, and Barton, Clough-Leighter, Fisher, Johns, Nevin and Spross were certainly like-minded in their approach. They took the Brahmsian strain of German music as their model, although they rarely reached the complexity of Brahms.

Ideologically opposed to them were the Wa-Wan Press composers: Ayres, Campbell-Tipton, Ide and especially Gilbert. They felt that American music was too German-sounding, by which they apparently meant too much like Brahms. Their music was much more chromatic; to my ears it leans toward Wagnerian harmony and thus still sounds Germanic, though it is indeed a definite departure from the Brahms school.

French influences began to be heard with Campbell-Tipton and even more strongly with Carpenter. As usual, Ives stands alone, or perhaps not far from Sousa, in the brash Americanism of "The Circus Band." Even in "Spring Song," where he seems to be trying to write in the prevailing sentimental idiom of the time, his humor overtakes him in the last two bars.

Carrie Jacobs Bond is harder to classify, but I couldn't resist her little moral lessons. Oley Speaks's "On the Road to Mandalay" used to be the staple of any baritone's American group or his best encore, as "Sylvia" was ubiquitous among tenors. Johns's "If Love Were Not" is in this collection because the last few lines have to be the funniest example I have ever seen of how to reverse the meaning of a poem. In the same spirit, I couldn't resist including Sousa's own words for his most famous march, which is much better off without them. Nevin's "Narcissus" was originally a piano solo, but it was so popular that it was arranged for every conceivable instrument; the text was grafted on by P. C. Warren, whoever he or she was.

There is no song here that I would not happily sing in concert. (I have recorded many of them for Albany Records on a CD called *Songs of an Innocent Age*, with Irma Vallecillo at the piano.) The Victorian era probably was not, in fact, any more innocent than ours, but the music sounds that way to us now after the complexities of the '60s and '70s. I hope that there are songs here for all tastes and for all singers, and that performers and audiences will derive as much pleasure as I do from these souvenirs of our past. Are they art songs or popular songs? It doesn't really matter; they are wonderful!

PAUL SPERRY

American Art Songs
of the
Turn of the Century

THREE SONGS, OP. 3

Take, O, Take Those Lips Away

William Shakespeare

Frederic Ayres

Take, O, take those lips a - way, That so sweet - ly were for - sworn; And those eyes, the break of day, Lights that do mis - lead the morn: But my kiss - es

bring a - gain; Seals of love, but seal'd in vain.

Seals of love, but seal'd in vain.

Where the Bee Sucks

William Shakespeare

Frederic Ayres

In a cow-slip's bell I lie; There I couch when owls do cry. There I couch when owls do cry.

On a bat's back do I fly___ af - ter sum - mer mer - ri - ly.___

Come unto These Yellow Sands

William Shakespeare

Frederic Ayres

Court - sied when you have and kissed, The wild waves whist:

Foot it feat - ly here and there; And, sweet sprites the bur - - - -

Poco Vivace.

- - - then bear. The

bur - - then bear.

It Was a Lover and His Lass

William Shakespeare

Gerard Barton

1. It
2. Be -
3. This
4. Then,

was a lov - er and his lass,
tween the a - cres of the rye,
car - ol they be - gan that hour,
pret - ty lov - ers, take the time,

With a hey, and a ho, and a

hey no - ni - no,

That o'er the green corn - fields did pass.
These pret - ty coun - try folks would lie,
How that a life was but a flow'r
For love is crown - ed with the prime

In

THREE BROWNING SONGS, OP. 44

The Year's at the Spring

Robert Browning

Amy Marcy Cheney Beach

The year's—at the spring,——— And day's—at the morn;——— —— Morn—ing's at sev—en; The hill — — side's dew — pearled;———

11

The year's — at the spring; — And day's — at the

morn; — The lark's — on the wing; — The

snail's on the thorn; — God's in his

Ah, Love, But a Day!

Robert Browning

Amy Marcy Cheney Beach

Lento con molto espressione.

Ah, Love, but a day,____ And the world has changed!____ Ah, Love, but a day,___ And the world____ has

I Send My Heart up to Thee!

Robert Browning

Amy Marcy Cheney Beach

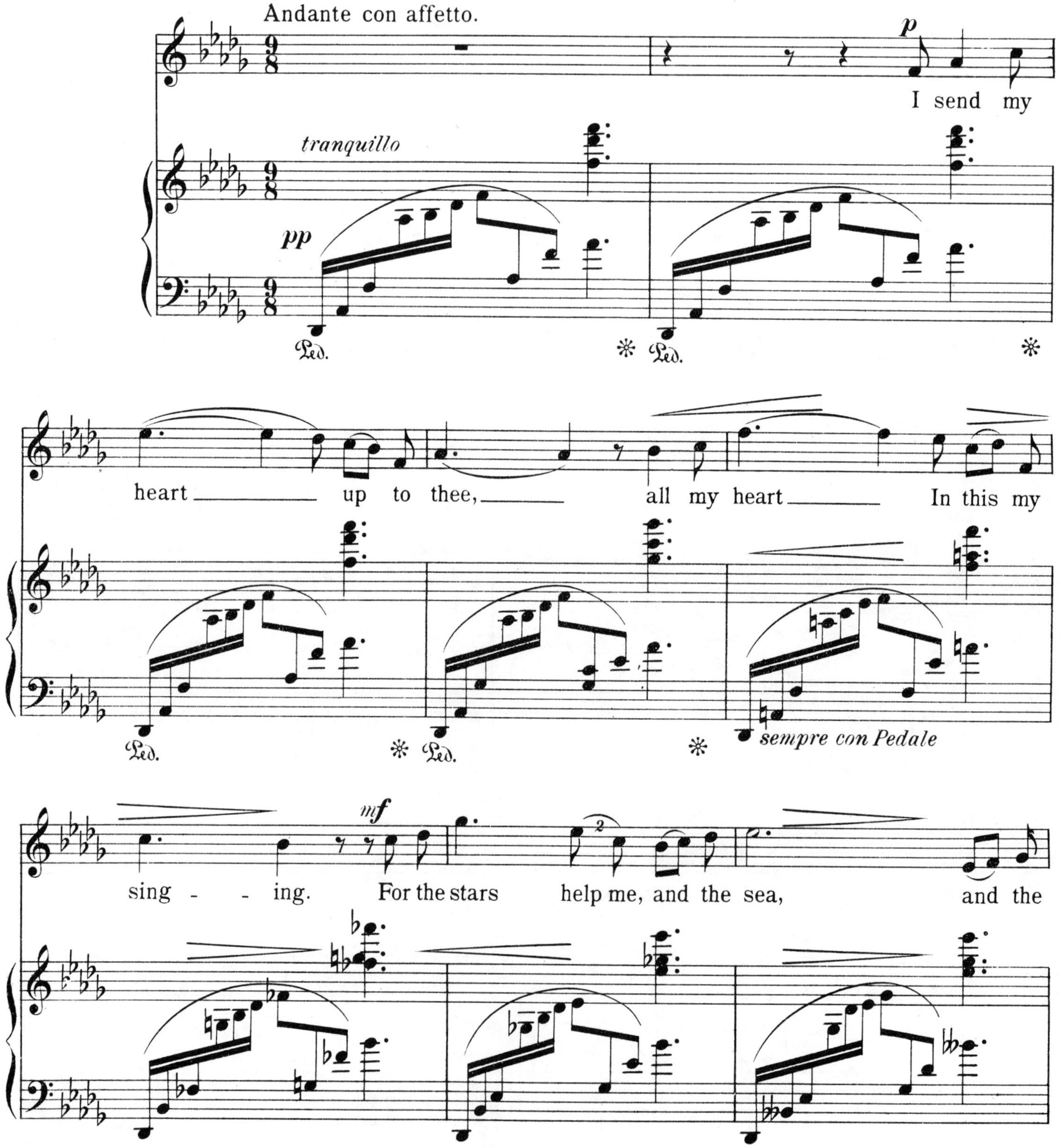

Andante con affetto.
p
I send my
tranquillo
pp
Ped.
heart up to thee, all my heart In this my
sempre con Pedale
sing - - ing. For the stars help me, and the sea, and the
mf

Half Minute Songs

Words and Music by Carrie Jacobs Bond

Making the Best of It.

What you can't help, what you can't help, what you can't help, for-get!

First Ask Yourself.

Before you have said it about them, Ask yourself if you'd like them to know you said it.

To Understand.

To understand a sorrow. You must have one all your own.

Doan' Yo' Lis'n.

No mattah w'at dey said, Keep a-walkin' straight ahaid. Wy, dey'll praise yo' when yo' daid. But doan' yo' lis-'n

How to Find Success.

The man who finds success. looks sometimes when he's tired. when he's tired. when he's tired, looks

sometimes when he's tired

The Pleasure of Giving

I'd rather say "You're welcome" once, than "Thank you" a thousand times.

Answer the First Rap.

Opportunity may knock often, but it's better to answer the first rap!

A Good Exercise.

With evil things you'll always find It's best to be deaf, dumb and blind.

A Present from Yourself.

A friend is a present you give yourself.

Now and Then.

The "luck-y" fel-low gets up at five (A.M.), and gen'rally works till ten (P.M.); But the other fellow, not quite so "lucky," works hard —— just now and then!

When They Say the Un-kind Things.

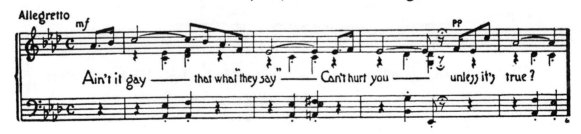

Ain't it gay —— that what "they say" —— Can't hurt you —— unless it's true?

Keep Awake.

Success never comes to the sleep-ing.

From the Land of the Sky-Blue Water

Nelle Richmond Eberhart

Charles Wakefield Cadman

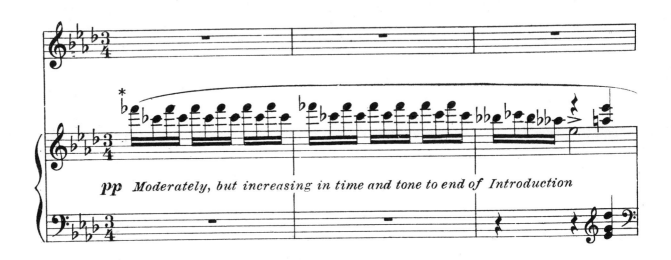

pp *Moderately, but increasing in time and tone to end of Introduction*

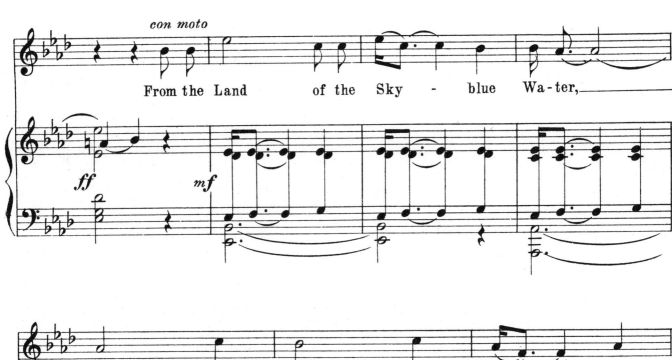

con moto

From the Land of the Sky - blue Wa-ter,_____

ff   mf

_____ They brought a cap - - tive

*Flageolet Love Call of the Omahas

28

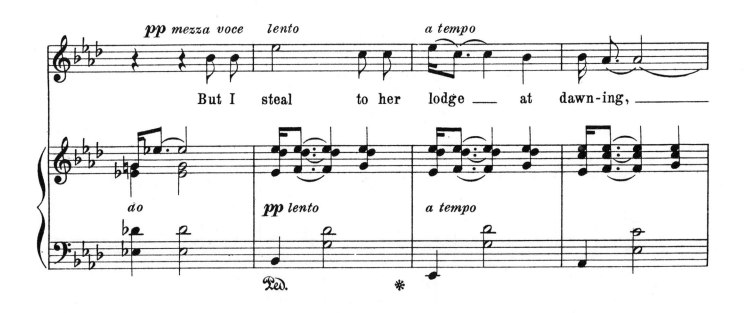

After Sunset

Arthur Symons

Louis Campbell-Tipton

Looking-Glass River

Robert Louis Stevenson

John Alden Carpenter

Les Silhouettes

Oscar Wilde

John Alden Carpenter

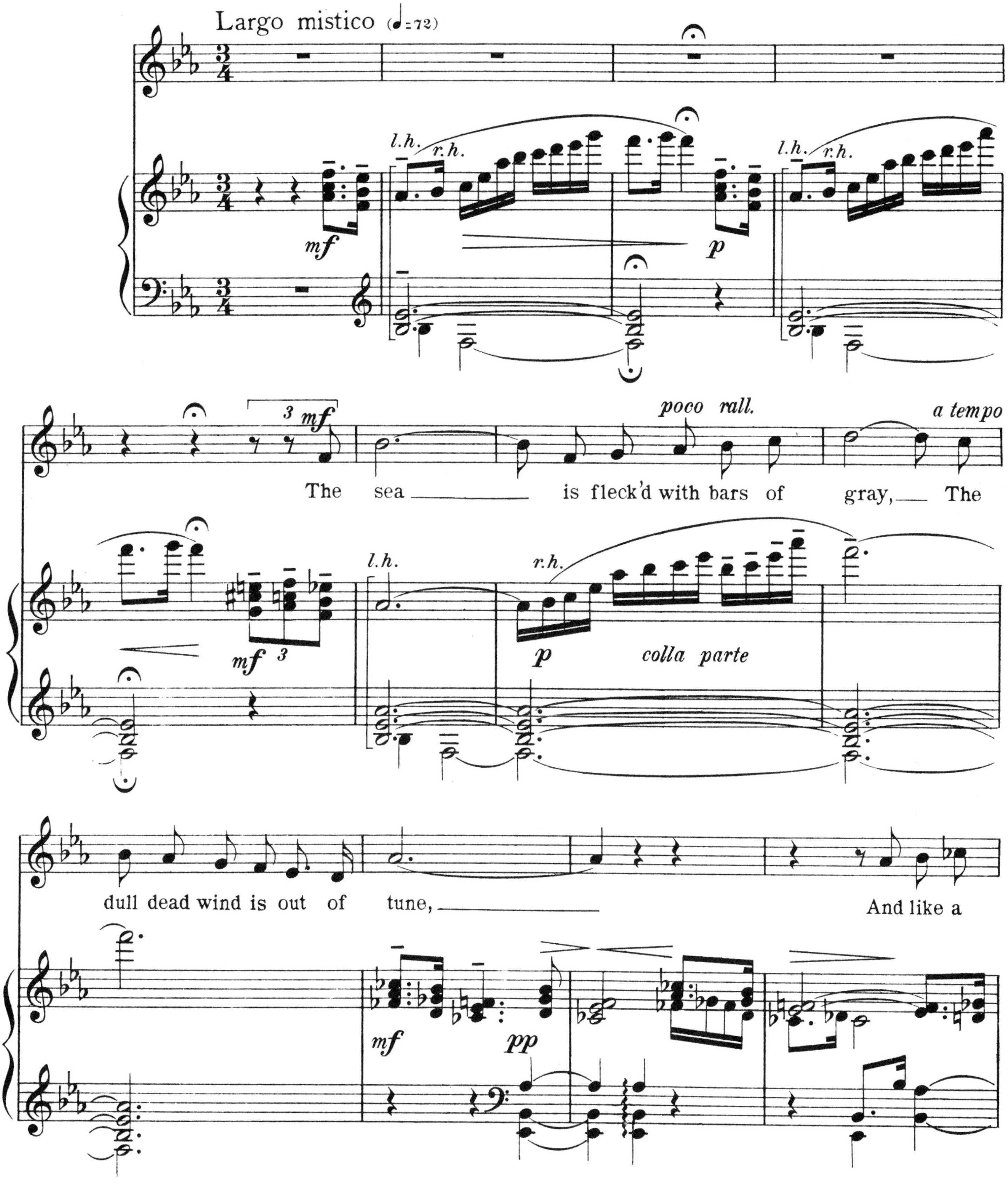

Largo mistico (♩=72)
l.h.
r.h.
mf
p
3
poco rall.
a tempo
The sea is fleck'd with bars of gray, The
colla parte
dull dead wind is out of tune,
And like a
pp

When I Bring to You Colour'd Toys

Rabindranath Tagore

John Alden Carpenter

44   *When I Bring to You Colour'd Toys*

When I sing to make you dance.____

When I bring sweet things to your greedy hands,____ I

know why there is hon-ey in the cup of the flower and why fruits are secretly

The Danza

Arlo Bates

George Whitefield Chadwick

Allegretto grazioso.

If you nev - er have danced...... The Dan - za............... with its won - drous rhyth-mic twirl........................ While close...... to your

Green Grows the Willow

Hamilton Aïdé

George Whitefield Chadwick

O I love my love the best, Green grows the wil-low, With the gold cross on her breast Ly-ing down to take her rest, On her green turf pil - - low.

Adversity

Arthur Macy

George Whitefield Chadwick

A soft eye's drooping lid,____ A witch-ing face,____ A snow-y breast half - hid,____ A bit of lace,____ Dear lips that sweet-ly smile____ A dream of bliss,____ And I, a lone____ ex - ile____ With-out a kiss.

The Stranger-Man

Arthur Macy

George Whitefield Chadwick

Now what is this, my_ daugh - ter dear, Up - on thy cheek so fair? 'Tis but a kiss, my moth-er dear, Kind for-tune sent it there; It was a courteous stran-ger-man That gave it un-to

here,   And   bid him hie   and bid him fly   To   me, my daugh - ter

dear;   For   times   be ver - y,   ver - y hard,   And

bless - ings eke so   rare,   I   fain   would   meet   a

stran - ger - man   That hath a kiss   to spare.

It Was a Lover and His Lass

William Shakespeare

Henry Clough-Leighter

Sigh No More, Ladies

William Shakespeare

William Arms Fisher

Men were de-ceiv-ers, Men were de-ceiv-ers, Men were de - ceiv-ers ev - er,
dumps dull and heav - y, dumps dull and heav - y; Of dumps so dull and heav-y,

To one thing con-stant nev-er: One foot in sea and one on shore, To
Since sum-mer first was leav-y The fraud of men was ev - er so, Since

one thing con-stant nev - er: }
sum-mer first was leav - y; } Then sigh not so, but let them go,

sigh not so, but let them go, And be you blithe and bon-ny, be you blithe and

bon-ny, Con -vert -ing all your sounds of_woe In -to Hey non-ny, non-ny, non-ny.

Sigh no more, la -dies, sigh no more, la -dies, Be you blithe and

bon-ny, be you blithe and bon-ny, Con -vert -ing_all your sounds of_woe In -to

Hey non-ny, non -ny, non-ny.

It Was a Lover and His Lass

William Shakespeare

Arthur Foote

o'er the green corn _ field did pass, In the spring _ time, the spring _ time, The
love is crown _ ed with the prime, In the spring _ time, the spring _ time, The

on _ ly pret _ ty ring _ time, When birds do sing hey ding a ding!

Sweet lov _ ers love the spring.

2$\underline{^{nd}}$ And Spring. (*Shakespeare.*)

Song of the Forge

Gilbert Parker

Arthur Foote

Allegro assai. (♩. = 104)

"Oh! tra - - veller, see where the red sparks rise!" (Fly a-

way___ my heart, fly a - way!)___ But dark is the mist in the

tra - veller's eyes;_ (Fly a - way___ my heart fly a - way!)___

"Oh! tra - veller, see, far down___ the gorge,___ The

crim - son light from my fa - ther's forge;" (Fly___ a -

way, my heart, fly a - way! Fly a - way, my heart, fly_ a -

O Swallow, Swallow, Flying South

Alfred Tennyson

Arthur Foote

The Owl

Alfred Tennyson

Henry F. Gilbert

lay, And the cock hath sung be - neath the thatch Twice or

thrice his round - e - lay; A - lone and warm - ing

a tempo ma allargando

ritenuto *a tempo ma allargando*

a tempo ma ritenuto molto e espressivo

his five wits, The white owl in _____ the bel - fry

a tempo ma ritenuto molto e espress.

sits. ___

p

Names

Samuel Taylor Coleridge

Chester E. Ide

Greece; La - la-ge, Ne - ae - ra, Chloris, Sap - pho, Les - bi - a, or Doris, Ar - e - thu-sa or Lu-crece. 'Ah!' re - plied my gen - tle fair, 'Be-lov - ed, what are names but air? Choose thou what - ev - er

cresc.

p *riten.*

f *p*

suits the line; Call__ me Sap-pho, call me Chlo-ris,

Call__ me La - la - ge or Do - ris, On - ly

on - ly call me thine!'_____

molto riten. *ff* *cresc.*

The Circus Band

Words and Music by Charles Ives

Where is___ the la - dy all in pink? Last

year she waved to me I think, Can she___ have died? Can! that! rot!

She___ is pass-ing but she sees me not.___

Spring Song

Harmony Twichell

Charles Ives

A - cross the hill of late, came spring____ and stopped and looked in - to this wood and called and called____ and called.

If Love Were Not

Florence Earle Coates

Clayton Johns

love were not, the wild-ing rose Would in its leaf-y heart en-close No

chal-ice of per fume; By moss-y bank, in glen or grot, No

THREE SONGS, OP. 60

Tyrant Love

Words and Music by Edward MacDowell

Lightly, yet with tenderness. (♩ =about 88.)

Where e'er Love be, Ty-rant he,____ With-out mer-ci;

Plead as thou may, Ah me! He ne'er thy tears will see, Ah me! Ah me!

Light wings hath he____ As an-y bee Let not him

98

Fair Springtide

Words and Music by Edward MacDowell

Very slow, with pathos. (♩=about 84.)

Fair Spring-tide com - - eth once a - gain ____

Stirs the sap in lone - ly trees ___ To wake a-gain the

bit-ter joy Of love _____ That mort - al eye ne'er sees, The

bit - ter joy of love___ Why wak _ _ en those___ who

sleep so sound ___ Why cause a - gain ___ the tears to

flow.___ Ah. Spring-tide thou dost touch the quick Of ev'_ ry crea_ture

here be - low. Ah Spring-tide! Ah Spring _ tide! Why wak- en those who

To the Golden Rod

Words and Music by Edward MacDowell

With tender grace. (♩.=about 52.)

A liss - ome maid with tows - eled hair As soft as e'er a squir - rel's vair, With ne'er a care, All silk - y fair, She sways to ev' - ry

woo - - - ing air. She

flaunts her gold - en gown with grace And laughs ____ in stur-dy

Aut - umn's face, A ray ___ of sun - shine in the race That

ends with hoar - y wint - - er's pace ____ With-

'Twas April!

Edouard Pailleron, trans. James Freeman Clark

Ethelbert Nevin

two lit - tle flow'rs were hid in your hair Yes; in your hair,_____

_____ On that day, gone by!_____

We sat on the moss: it was

sha - dy and dry, Yes! sha - dy and dry; We sat in the shad - ow, We

Narcissus

P. C. Warren

Ethelbert Nevin

A Song of Love

Edmond Lock Tomlin

Ethelbert Nevin

saw a weep-ing maid-en A — search-ing in the morn For

Love, that's half a rose-bud, For Love, that's half a thorn. She

hid in fern-y for - est, The dar - ling of her dream.   He

lurked not in the pop - pies, He shone not in the sky;   But

called to her from out my heart, And yet she passed him by!

Early Spring Time

Rev. Thomas Hill

John Knowles Paine

Lute-Song

Alfred Tennyson

Horatio Parker

Hap-less doom of wo-man,

Hap - py in be-troth-ing, Beau-ty pass-es like a breath, And

love is lost in loath-ing. Low, my lute, speak low, my lute, But

say the world is no-thing. Low, lute, low!

Low, lute, low!

Love will hov - er round the flow'rs

The Blackbird

William Ernest Henley

Horatio Parker

sung_ Our_ hearts and lips to - geth - er. _

The blackbird plays but a box-wood flute, but a

box - wood flute, But I love_ him_ best of all.

Reveille

Robert J. Burdette

John Philip Sousa

can't get 'em up, I can't get 'em up, I can't get 'em up, I can't get 'em up" Ring

out the cheer - y bu — gle call............ Through

wood - ed vale, ... o'er wind-swept hill, ... Where camp-

fires gleam and shad - ows fall, ... And

You'll Miss Lots of Fun When You're Married

Edward M. Taber

John Philip Sousa

Valse Grazioso.

Mat - ri -
Now

mo - ni - al life is pro - duc - tive of bliss,   As
what   could be sweet - er   and bet - ter in   life   Than a-

an - y sane man will ad - mit. . . . .   And
void - ing its wea - ry tur - moil, ...   And he

he   who don't seek   it   is   sure - ly   re - miss,   And
wel - comed at home   by   your   own   lit - tle wife,   When you've

has   neith - er wis - dom nor   wit. . . . .   For
fin - ished your di - ur - nal   toil. . . . .   Of

when   a   man's sin - gle,   he'll   find   life   is   bleak,   A
course you must   give   up   your   bach - el - or   ways.   And the

des - ert that's bar - ren and   ar - id, ...   And
style that you   al - ways have car - ried, ...   And

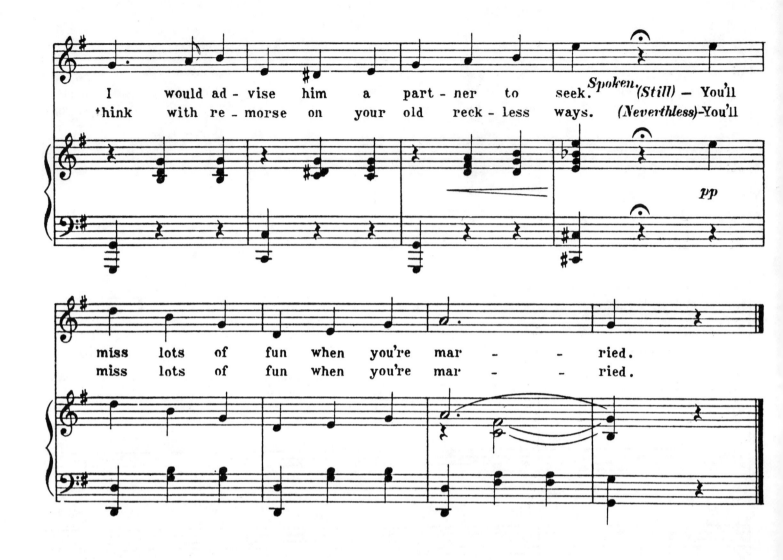

I would ad - vise him a part - ner to seek. *Spoken. (Still)* — You'll
think with re - morse on your old reck - less ways. *(Neverthless)*-You'll

miss lots of fun when you're mar - ried.
miss lots of fun when you're mar - ried.

pp

3.

O why should a man seek to fresco the town,
  Or stay out all night and play draw,
When he at his home might sit peacefully down,
  And converse with his mother-in-law.
For love and contentment are better by far
  Than a conscience by wickedness harried,
And unhappy, therefore, all bachelors are,
  Spoken.(Notwithstanding which, however,)—
You'll miss lots of fun when you're married.

4.

Now please do not think for a moment, my friends,
  This is a satirical song,
Or that in its sentiments anything tends
  To views that are worldly or wrong.
For when you are wed you so happy will be
  You will wish you had not so long tarried,
And then, I suppose, you will villify me,
  Spoken. (But, all the same,) —
You'll miss lots of fun when you're married.

The Stars and Stripes Forever!

Words and Music by John Philip Sousa

ban-ner of the West-ern - land.   The em - blem of   the brave   and true, Its
ech- o of the chor-us   grand.   Sing   out   for lib - er - ty   and light, Sing

folds   pro -tect   no   ty - rant crew,   The   red   and white   and
out   for free - dom and   the right,   Sing   out   for Un - - ion

star - ry blue, Is Free - dom's shield   and   hope.⎫   Oth - er
and   its might, Oh, pa - -tri - ot - - ic   Sons!⎭

na - tions may deem their flags the best And cheer them with fer - vid e -

la - - tion, But the flag of the North and South and West Is the

CHORUS.

flag of flags, The flag of Free-dom's na - - tion. Hur - rah for the flag of the

free, May it wave as our stand - ard for - ev - - er, The

On the Road to Mandalay

Rudyard Kipling

Oley Speaks

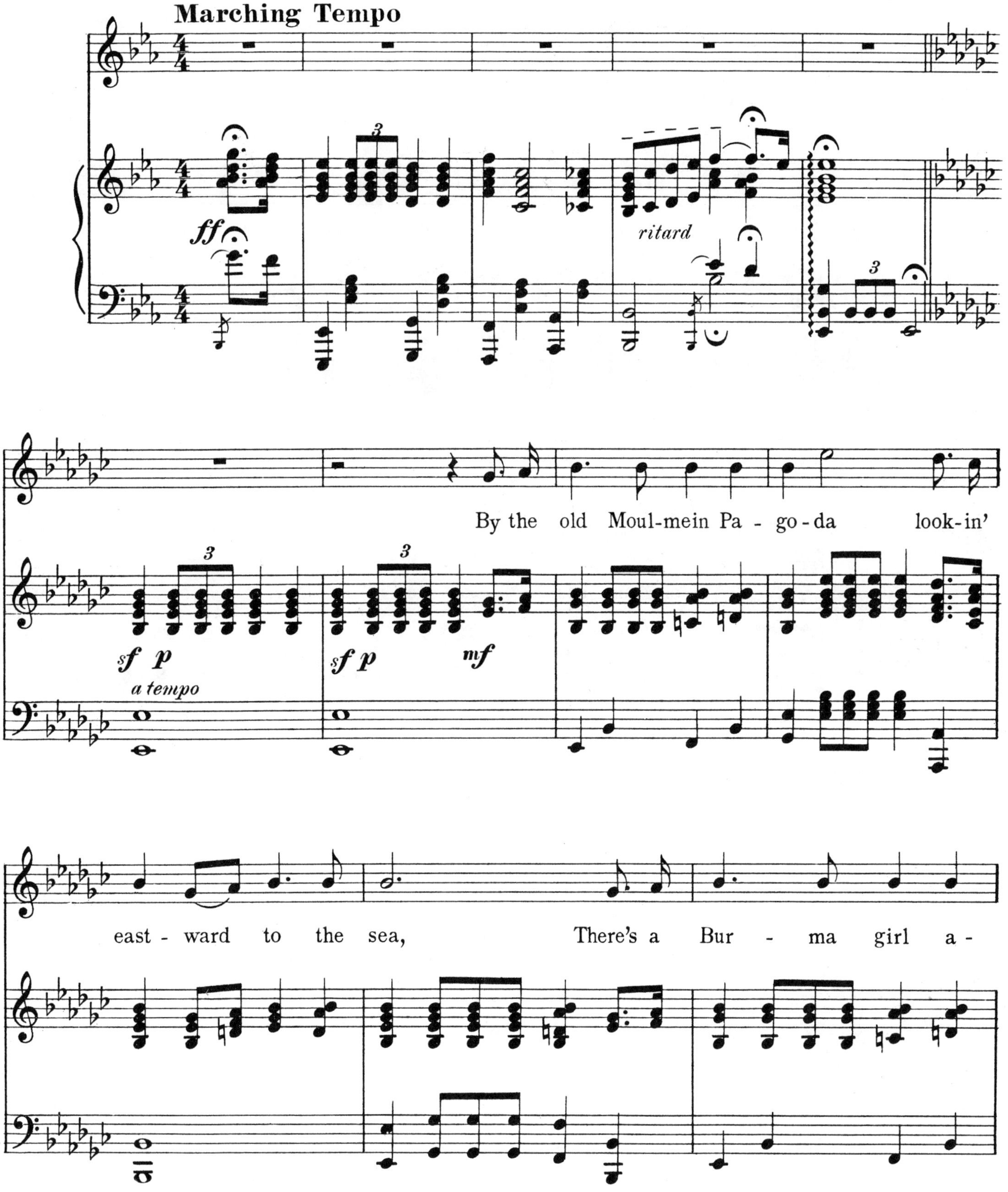

Marching Tempo
ff
ritard
sf p
a tempo
sf p
mf
By the old Moul-mein Pa - go-da look-in'
east - ward to the sea, There's a Bur - ma girl a -

set-tin' and I know she thinks of me. For the wind is in the palm-trees, and the tem - ple bells they say, "Come you back, you Brit - ish sol-dier, Come you back to Man-da - lay," Come you back to Man-da - lay. Come you back to Man-da -

there that I would be, By the old Moul-mein Pa-

go-da look-in' la - zy at the sea, look-in'

la - zy at the sea. Come you back to Man-da-

lay, where the old Flo - - til - la lay, Can't you

'ear their pad - dles chunk - in' from Ran - goon to Man - da -

lay? On the road to Man - da - lay___ where the

fly - in' fish - es play An' the dawn comes up like

thun - der out of Chi - na 'crost the bay.

Sylvia

Clinton Scollard

Oley Speaks

Syl-via's hair is like the night, Touched with glanc-ing star-ry beams;

Such a face as drifts thro' dreams, This is Syl-via to the sight.

And the touch of Syl - via's hand Is as light as milk - weed down,

When the meads are gold - en brown,___ And the au - tumn fills the

land._____

Syl - via:- just the e - cho - ing Of her voice brings back to me,

Will o' the Wisp

Torrence Benjamin

Charles Gilbert Spross

Will · o'- the-wisp with your dan - cing light, Where do you wan-der in -to the night?

Where will you lead, if I keep you in sight?

Will - o'-the-wisp,

Will your lan - tern il - lu-mine for me A fair - y ring 'neath a

for - est tree? Or will you beckon me down to the sea?

Will - o'-the-wisp.

Dover Piano and Keyboard Editions

ORGAN WORKS, César Franck. Composer's best-known works for organ, including Six Pieces, Trois Pieces, and Trois Chorals. Oblong format for easy use at keyboard. Authoritative Durand edition. 208pp. 11⅜ × 8¼. 25517-4 Pa. **$9.95**

IBERIA AND ESPAÑA: Two Complete Works for Solo Piano, Isaac Albeniz. Spanish composer's greatest piano works in authoritative editions. Includes the popular "Tango". 192pp. 9 × 12. 25367-8 Pa. **$9.95**

GOYESCAS, SPANISH DANCES AND OTHER WORKS FOR SOLO PIANO, Enrique Granados. Great Spanish composer's most admired, most performed suites for the piano, in definitive Spanish editions. 176pp. 9 × 12. 25481-X Pa. **$7.95**

SELECTED PIANO COMPOSITIONS, César Franck, edited by **Vincent d'Indy.** Outstanding selection of influential French composer's piano works, including early pieces and the two masterpieces—Prelude, Choral and Fugue; and Prelude, Aria and Finale. Ten works in all. 138pp. 9 × 12. 23269-7 Pa. **$8.95**

THE COMPLETE PRELUDES AND ETUDES FOR PIANOFORTE SOLO, Alexander Scriabin. All the preludes and études including many perfectly spun miniatures. Edited by K. N. Igumnov and Y. I. Mil'shteyn. 250pp. 9 × 12. 22919-X Pa. **$9.95**

COMPLETE PIANO SONATAS, Alexander Scriabin. All ten of Scriabin's sonatas, reprinted from an authoritative early Russian edition. 256pp. 8⅜ × 11¼. 25850-5 Pa. **$9.95**

COMPLETE PRELUDES AND ETUDES-TABLEAUX, Serge Rachmaninoff. Forty-one of his greatest works for solo piano, including the riveting C minor, G-minor and B-minor preludes, in authoritative editions. 208pp. 8⅜ × 11¼. (Available in U.S. only) 25696-0 Pa. **$9.95**

COMPLETE PIANO SONATAS, Sergei Prokofiev. Definitive Russian edition of nine sonatas (1907–1953), among the most important compositions in the modern piano repertoire. 288pp. 8⅜ × 11¼. (Available in U.S. only) 25689-8 Pa. **$10.95**

GYMNOPEDIES, GNOSSIENNES AND OTHER WORKS FOR PIANO, Erik Satie. The largest Satie collection of piano works yet published, 17 in all, reprinted from the original French editions. 176pp. 9 × 12. 25978-1 Pa. **$8.95**

TWENTY SHORT PIECES FOR PIANO (Sports et Divertissements), Erik Satie. French master's brilliant thumbnail sketches—verbal and musical—of various outdoor sports and amusements. English translations, 20 illustrations. Rare, limited 1925 edition. 48pp. 12 × 8⅞. 24365-6 Pa. **$4.95**

COMPLETE PRELUDES, IMPROMPTUS AND VALSES-CAPRICES, Gabriel Fauré. Eighteen elegantly wrought piano works in authoritative editions. Only one-volume collection. 144pp. 9 × 12. 25789-4 Pa. **$7.95**

PIANO MUSIC OF BÉLA BARTÓK, Series I, Béla Bartók. New, definitive Archive Edition incorporating composer's corrections. Includes *Funeral March* from *Kossuth, Fourteen Bagatelles,* Bartók's break to modernism. 167pp. 9 × 12. (Available in U.S. only) 24108-4 Pa. **$9.95**

PIANO MUSIC OF BÉLA BARTÓK, Series II, Béla Bartók. Second in the Archie Edition incorporating composer's corrections. 85 short pieces *For Children, Two Elegies, Two Rumanian Dances,* etc. 192pp. 9 × 12. (Available in U.S. only) 24109-2 Pa. **$9.95**

FRENCH PIANO MUSIC, AN ANTHOLOGY, edited by **Isidor Phillipp.** 44 complete works, 1670–1905, by Lully, Couperin, Rameau, Alkan, Saint-Saëns, Delibes, Bizet, Godard, many others; favorites, lesser-known examples, but all top quality. 188pp. 9 × 12. 23381-2 Pa. **$8.95**

NINETEENTH-CENTURY EUROPEAN PIANO MUSIC: UNFAMILIAR MASTERWORKS, edited by **John Gillespie.** Difficult-to-find études, toccatas, polkas, impromptus, waltzes, etc., by Albéniz, Bizet, Chabrier, Fauré, Smetana, Richard Strauss, Wagner and 16 other composers. 62 pieces. 343pp. 9 × 12. 23447-9 Pa. **$13.95**

RARE MASTERPIECES OF RUSSIAN PIANO MUSIC: Eleven Pieces by Glinka, Balakirev, Glazunov and Others, edited by **Dmitry Feofanov.** Glinka's *Prayer,* Balakirev's *Reverie,* Liapunov's *Transcendental Etude, Op. 11, No. 10,* and eight others—full, authoritative scores from Russian texts. 144pp. 9 × 12. 24659-0 Pa. **$7.95**

NINETEENTH-CENTURY AMERICAN PIANO MUSIC, edited by **John Gillespie.** 40 pieces by 27 American composers: Gottschalk, Victor Herbert, Edward MacDowell, William Mason, Ethelbert Nevin, others. 323pp. 9 × 12. 23602-1 Pa. **$14.95**

PIANO MUSIC, Louis M. Gottschalk. 26 pieces (including covers) by early 19th-century American genius. "Bamboula," "The Banjo," other Creole, Negro-based material, through elegant salon music. 301pp. 9¼ × 12. 21683-7 Pa. **$12.95**

SOUSA'S GREAT MARCHES IN PIANO TRANSCRIPTION, John Philip Sousa. Playing edition includes: "The Stars and Stripes Forever," "King Cotton," "Washington Post," much more. 24 illustrations. 111pp. 9 × 12. 23132-1 Pa. **$5.95**

COMPLETE PIANO RAGS, Scott Joplin. All 38 piano rags by the acknowledged master of the form, reprinted from the publisher's original editions complete with sheet music covers. Introduction by David A. Jasen. 208pp. 9 × 12. 25807-6 Pa. **$8.95**

RAGTIME REDISCOVERIES, selected by **Trebor Jay Tichenor.** 64 unusual rags demonstrate diversity of style, local tradition. Original sheet music. 320pp. 9 × 12. 23776-1 Pa. **$11.95**

RAGTIME RARITIES, edited by **Trebor J. Tichenor.** 63 tuneful, rediscovered piano rags by 51 composers (or teams). Does not duplicate selections in *Classic Piano Rags* (Dover, 20469-3). 305pp. 9 × 12. 23157-7 Pa. **$12.95**

CLASSIC PIANO RAGS, selected with an introduction by **Rudi Blesh.** Best ragtime music (1897–1922) by Scott Joplin, James Scott, Joseph F. Lamb, Tom Turpin, nine others. 364pp. 9 × 12. 20469-3 Pa. **$14.95**

RAGTIME GEMS: Original Sheet Music for 25 Ragtime Classics, edited by **David A. Jasen.** Includes original sheet music and covers for 25 rags, including three of Scott Joplin's finest: *Searchlight Rag, Rose Leaf Rag* and *Fig Leaf Rag.* 122pp. 9 × 12. 25248-5 Pa. **$7.95**

LEROY ANDERSON: 25 GREAT MELODIES FOR PIANO SOLO, Leroy Anderson. Delightful collection of favorites: "Blue Tango," "The Syncopated Clock," "Sleigh Ride," others. Easily playable by intermediate-level pianists. 121pp. 9 × 11⅞. 24067-3 Pa. **$14.95**

ZEZ CONFREY PIANO SOLOS, RAGTIME, NOVELTY & JAZZ, Belwin Mills. 90 great hits of famed piano composer: "Kitten on the Keys," "Dizzy Fingers," "Giddy Ditty," many others. 329pp. 9 × 12. 24681-7 Pa. **$22.50**

MY VERY FIRST BOOK OF COWBOY SONGS, Dolly Moon. 21 favorites arranged for little hands. "Red River Valley," "My Darling Clementine," 19 more. Illustrated with Remington prints. 46pp. 8¼ × 11. 24311-7 Pa. **$3.50**

SELECTED PIANO WORKS FOR FOUR HANDS, Franz Schubert. 24 separate pieces (16 most popular titles): Three Military Marches, Lebensstürme, Four Polonaises, Four Ländler, etc. Rehearsal numbers added. 273pp. 9 × 12. 23529-7 Pa. **$10.95**

Available from your music dealer or write for free Music Catalog to
Dover Publications, Inc., Dept. MUBI, 31 East 2nd Street, Mineola, N.Y. 11501.

Dover Opera, Choral and Lieder Scores

ELEVEN GREAT CANTATAS, J. S. Bach. Full vocal-instrumental score from Bach-Gesellschaft edition. *Christ lag in Todesbanden, Ich hatte viel Bekümmerniss, Jauchhzet Gott in allen Landen*, eight others. Study score. 350pp. 9 × 12.   23268-9 Pa. **$13.95**

SEVEN GREAT SACRED CANTATAS IN FULL SCORE, Johann Sebastian Bach. Seven favorite sacred cantatas. Printed from a clear, modern engraving and sturdily bound; new literal line-for-line translations. Reliable Bach-Gesellschaft edition. Complete German texts. 256pp. 9 × 12.   24950-6 Pa. **$10.95**

SIX GREAT SECULAR CANTATAS IN FULL SCORE, Johann Sebastian Bach. Bach's nearest approach to comic opera. *Hunting Cantata, Wedding Cantata, Aeolus Appeased, Phoebus and Pan, Coffee Cantata*, and *Peasant Cantata*. 286pp. 9 × 12.   23934-9 Pa. **$11.95**

MASS IN B MINOR IN FULL SCORE, Johann Sebastian Bach. The crowning glory of Bach's lifework in the field of sacred music and a universal statement of Christian faith, reprinted from the authoritative Bach-Gesellschaft edition. Translation of texts. 320pp. 9 × 12.
25992-7 Pa. **$12.95**

GIULIO CESARE IN FULL SCORE, George Frideric Handel. Great Baroque masterpiece reproduced directly from authoritative Deutsche Handelgesellschaft edition. Gorgeous melodies, inspired orchestration. Complete and unabridged. 160pp. 9⅜ × 12¼.   25056-3 Pa. **$8.95**

MESSIAH IN FULL SCORE, George Frideric Handel. An authoritative full-score edition of the oratorio that is the best-known, most beloved, most performed large-scale musical work in the English-speaking world. 240pp. 9 × 12.   26067-4 Pa. **$10.95**

REQUIEM IN FULL SCORE, Wolfgang Amadeus Mozart. Masterpiece of vocal composition, among the most recorded and performed works in the repertoire. Authoritative edition published by Breitkopf & Härtel, Wiesbaden, n.d. 203pp. 8⅜ × 11¼.   25311-2 Pa. **$6.95**

COSI FAN TUTTE IN FULL SCORE, Wolfgang Amadeus Mozart. Scholarly edition of one of Mozart's greatest operas. Da Ponte libretto. Commentary. Preface. Translated frontmatter. 448pp. 9⅜ × 12¼. (Available in U.S. only)   24528-4 Pa. **$16.95**

THE MARRIAGE OF FIGARO: COMPLETE SCORE, Wolfgang A. Mozart. Finest comic opera ever written. Full score, not to be confused with piano renderings. Peters edition. Study score. 448pp. 9⅜ × 12¼. (Available in U.S. only)   23751-6 Pa. **$16.95**

DON GIOVANNI: COMPLETE ORCHESTRAL SCORE, Wolfgang A. Mozart. Full score, not to be confused with piano reductions. All optional numbers, much material not elsewhere. Peters edition. Study score. 468pp. 9⅜ × 12¼. (Available in U.S. only)   23026-0 Pa. **$16.95**

THE ABDUCTION FROM THE SERAGLIO IN FULL SCORE, Wolfgang Amadeus Mozart. Mozart's early comic masterpiece, exactingly reproduced from the authoritative Breitkopf & Härtel edition. 320pp. 9 × 12.   **26004-6 Pa. $12.95**

THE MAGIC FLUTE (DIE ZAUBERFLÖTE) IN FULL SCORE, Wolfgang Amadeus Mozart. Authoritative C. F. Peters edition of Mozart's last opera featuring all the spoken dialogue. Translation of German frontmatter. Dramatis personae. List of Numbers. 226pp. 9 × 12.   24783-X Pa. **$10.95**

THE SEASONS IN FULL SCORE, Joseph Haydn. A masterful coda to a prolific career, this brilliant oratorio—Haydn's last major work. Unabridged republication of the work as published by C. F. Peters, Leipzig, n.d. English translation of frontmatter. 320pp. 9 × 12.
25022-9 Pa. **$12.95**

FIDELIO IN FULL SCORE, Ludwig van Beethoven. Beethoven's only opera, complete in one affordable volume, including all spoken German dialogue. Republication of C. F. Peters, Leipzig edition. 272pp. 9 × 12.   24740-6 Pa. **$12.95**

THE BARBER OF SEVILLE IN FULL SCORE, Gioacchino Rossini. One of the greatest comic operas ever written, reproduced here directly from the authoritative score published by Ricordi. 464pp. 8⅜ × 11¼.   26019-4 Pa. **$15.95**

GERMAN REQUIEM IN FULL SCORE, Johannes Brahms. Definitive Breitkopf & Härtel edition of Brahms's greatest vocal work, fully scored for solo voices, mixed chorus and orchestra. 208pp. 9⅜ × 12¼.   25486-0 Pa. **$9.95**

REQUIEM IN FULL SCORE, Giuseppe Verdi. Immensely popular with choral groups and music lovers. Republication of edition published by C. F. Peters, Leipzig, n.d. Study score. 204pp. 9⅜ × 12¼. (Available in U.S. only)   23682-X Pa. **$9.95**

OTELLO IN FULL SCORE, Giuseppe Verdi. The penultimate Verdi opera, his tragic masterpiece. Complete unabridged score from authoritative Ricordi edition, with frontmatter translated. 576pp. 8¼ × 11.   25040-7 Pa. **$18.95**

FALSTAFF, Giuseppe Verdi. Verdi's last great work, first and only comedy. Complete unabridged score from original Ricordi edition. 480pp. 8⅜ × 11¼.   24017-7 Pa. **$14.95**

AÏDA IN FULL SCORE, Giuseppe Verdi. Verdi's most popular opera in an authoritative edition from G. Ricordi of Milan. 448pp. 9 × 12.   26172-7 Pa. **$16.95**

LA BOHÈME IN FULL SCORE, Giacomo Puccini. Authoritative Italian edition of one of the world's most beloved operas. English translations of list of characters and instruments. 416pp. 8⅜ × 11¼.   25477-1 Pa. **$16.95**

DER FREISCHÜTZ, Carl Maria von Weber. Full orchestral score to first Romantic opera, path-breaker for later developments, Wagner. Still very popular. Study score, including full spoken text. 203pp. 9 × 12.   23449-5 Pa. **$8.95**

CARMEN IN FULL SCORE, Georges Bizet. Complete, authoritative score of what is perhaps the world's most popular opera, in the version most commonly performed today, with recitatives by Ernest Guiraud. 574pp. 9 × 12.   25820-3 Pa. **$19.95**

DAS RHEINGOLD IN FULL SCORE, Richard Wagner. Complete score, clearly reproduced from authoritative B. Schott's edition. New translation of German frontmatter. 328pp. 9 × 12.   24925-5 Pa. **$13.95**

DIE WALKÜRE, Richard Wagner. Complete orchestral score of the most popular of the operas in the Ring Cycle. Reprint of the edition published in Leipzig by C. F. Peters, ca. 1910. Study score. 710pp. 8⅜ × 11¼.   23566-1 Pa. **$23.95**

SIEGFRIED IN FULL SCORE, Richard Wagner. *Siegfried*, third opera of Wagner's famous *Ring*, is reproduced from first edition (1876). 439pp. 9⅜ × 12¼.   24456-3 Pa. **$16.95**

GÖTTERDÄMMERUNG, Richard Wagner. Full operatic score available in U.S. for the first time. Reprinted directly from rare 1877 first edition. 615pp. 9⅜ × 12¼.   24250-1 Pa. **$22.95**

DIE MEISTERSINGER VON NÜRNBERG, Richard Wagner. Landmark in history of opera in complete vocal and orchestral score. Do not confuse with piano reduction. Peters, Leipzig edition. Study score. 823pp. 8⅜ × 11.   23276-X Pa. **$24.95**

---

*Available from your music dealer or write for **free** Music Catalog to
Dover Publications, Inc., Dept. MUBI, 31 East 2nd Street, Mineola, N.Y. 11501.*

Dover Opera, Choral and Lieder Scores

LOHENGRIN IN FULL SCORE, Richard Wagner. Wagner's most accessible opera. Reproduced from first engraved edition (Breitkopf & Härtel, 1887). 295pp. 9⅜ × 12¼.   24335-4 Pa. **$15.95**

TANNHÄUSER IN FULL SCORE, Richard Wagner. Reproduces the original 1845 full orchestral and vocal score as slightly amended in 1847. Included is the ballet music for Act I written for the 1861 Paris production. 576pp. 8⅜ × 11¼.   24649-3 Pa. **$18.95**

TRISTAN UND ISOLDE, Richard Wagner. Full orchestral score with complete instrumentation. Study score. 655pp. 8⅛ × 11.   22915-7 Pa. **$21.95**

PARSIFAL IN FULL SCORE, Richard Wagner. Composer's deeply personal treatment of the legend of the Holy Grail, renowned for splendid music, glowing orchestration. C. F. Peters edition. 592pp. 8⅛ × 11.   25175-6 Pa. **$17.95**

THE FLYING DUTCHMAN IN FULL SCORE, Richard Wagner. Great early masterpiece reproduced directly from limited Weingartner edition (1896), incorporating Wagner's revisions. Text, stage directions in English, German, Italian. 432pp. 9⅜ × 12¼.   25629-4 Pa. **$16.95**

BORIS GODUNOV IN FULL SCORE (Rimsky-Korsakov Version), Modest Petrovich Moussorgsky. Russian operatic masterwork in most recorded, performed version. Authoritative Moscow edition. 784pp. 8⅜ × 11¼.   25321-X Pa. **$29.95**

PELLÉAS ET MÉLISANDE IN FULL SCORE, Claude Debussy. Reprinted from the E. Fromont (1904) edition, this volume faithfully reproduces the full orchestral-vocal score of Debussy's sole and enduring opera masterpiece. 416pp. 9 × 12. (Available in U.S. only)   24825-9 Pa. **$15.95**

SALOME IN FULL SCORE, Richard Strauss. Atmospheric color predominates in basic 20th-century work. Definitive Fürstner score, now extremely rare. 352pp. 9⅜ × 12¼. (Available in U.S. only)   24208-0 Pa. **$14.95**

DER ROSENKAVALIER IN FULL SCORE, Richard Strauss. First inexpensive edition of great operatic masterpiece, reprinted complete and unabridged from rare, limited Fürstner edition (1910) approved by Strauss. 528pp. 9⅜ × 12¼. (Available in U.S. only)   25498-4 Pa. **$19.95**

DER ROSENKAVALIER: VOCAL SCORE, Richard Strauss. Inexpensive edition reprinted directly from original Fürstner (1911) edition of vocal score. Verbal text, vocal line and piano "reduction." 448pp. 8⅜ × 11¼. (Available in U.S. only)   25501-8 Pa. **$14.95**

THE MERRY WIDOW: Complete Score for Piano and Voice in English, Franz Lehar. Complete score for piano and voice, reprinted directly from the first English translation (1907) published by Chappell & Co., London. 224pp. 8⅜ × 11¼. (Available in U.S. only)   24514-4 Pa. **$9.95**

THE AUTHENTIC GILBERT & SULLIVAN SONGBOOK, W. S. Gilbert, A. S. Sullivan. 92 songs, uncut, original keys, in piano renderings approved by Sullivan. 399pp. 9 × 12.   23482-7 Pa. **$14.95**

MADRIGALS: BOOK IV & V, Claudio Monteverdi. 39 finest madrigals with new English line-for-line literal translations of the poems facing the Italian text. 256pp. 8⅛ × 11. (Available in U.S. only)   25102-0 Pa. **$12.95**

COMPLETE SONG CYCLES, Franz Schubert. Complete piano, vocal music of *Die Schöne Müllerin, Die Winterreise, Schwanengesang.* Also Drinker English singing translations. Breitkopf & Härtel edition. 217pp. 9⅜ × 12¼.   22649-2 Pa. **$9.95**

SCHUBERT'S SONGS TO TEXTS BY GOETHE, Franz Schubert. Only one-volume edition of Schubert's Goethe songs from authoritative Breitkopf & Härtel edition, plus all revised versions. New prose translation of poems. 84 songs. 256pp. 9⅜ × 12¼.   23752-4 Pa. **$11.95**

59 FAVORITE SONGS, Franz Schubert. "Der Wanderer," "Ave Maria," "Hark, Hark, the Lark," and 56 other masterpieces of lieder reproduced from the Breitkopf & Härtel edition. 256pp. 9⅜ × 12¼.   24849-6 Pa. **$9.95**

SONGS FOR SOLO VOICE AND PIANO, Ludwig van Beethoven. 71 lieder, including "Adelaide," "Wonne der Wehmuth," "Die ehre Gottes aus der Natur," and famous cycle *An die ferne Geliebta.* Breitkopf & Härtel edition. 192pp. 9 × 12.   25125-X Pa. **$9.95**

SELECTED SONGS FOR SOLO VOICE AND PIANO, Robert Schumann. Over 100 of Schumann's greatest lieder, set to poems by Heine, Goethe, Byron, others. Breitkopf & Härtel edition. 248pp. 9⅜ × 12¼.   24202-1 Pa. **$10.95**

THIRTY SONGS, Franz Liszt. Selection of extremely worthwhile though not widely-known songs. Texts in French, German, and Italian, all with English translations. Piano, high voice. 144pp. 9 × 12.   23197-6 Pa. **$7.95**

OFFENBACH'S SONGS FROM THE GREAT OPERETTAS, Jacques Offenbach. Piano, vocal (French text) for 38 most popular songs: *Orphée, Belle Héléne, Vie Parisienne, Duchesse de Gérolstein,* others. 21 illustrations. 195pp. 9 × 12.   23341-3 Pa. **$9.95**

SONGS, 1880–1904, Claude Debussy. Rich selection of 36 songs set to texts by Verlaine, Baudelaire, Pierre Louys, Charles d'Orleans, others. 175pp. 9 × 12.   24131-9 Pa. **$8.95**

THE COMPLETE MÖRIKE SONGS, Hugo Wolf. Splendid settings of 53 poems by Eduard Mörike. "Der Tambour," "Elfenlied," "Verborganheit," 50 more. New prose translations. 208pp. 9⅜ × 12¼.   24380-X Pa. **$11.95**

SPANISH AND ITALIAN SONGBOOKS, Hugo Wolf. Total of 90 songs by great 19th-century master of the genre. Reprint of authoritative C. F. Peters edition. New Translations of German texts. 256pp. 9⅜ × 12¼.   26156-5 Pa. **$11.95**

SIXTY SONGS, Gabriel Fauré. "Clair de lune," "Apres un reve," "Chanson du pecheur," "Automne," and other great songs set for medium voice. Reprinted from French editions. 288pp. 8⅜ × 11.   26534-X Pa. **$13.95**

FRENCH ART SONGS OF THE NINETEENTH-CENTURY, edited by Philip Hale. 39 songs from romantic period by 18 composers: Berlioz, Chausson, Debussy (six songs), Gounod, Massenet, Thomas, etc. For high voice, French text, English singing translation. 182pp. 9 × 12.   23680-3 Pa. **$8.95**

COMPLETE SONGS FOR SOLO VOICE AND PIANO (two volumes), Johannes Brahms. A total of 113 songs in complete score by greatest lieder writer since Schubert. Volume I contains 15-song cycle Die Schone Magelone; Volume II famous "Lullaby." Total of 448pp. 9⅜ × 12¼.   Volume I 23820-2 Pa. **$9.95**   Volume II 23821-0 Pa. **$9.95**

COMPLETE SONGS FOR SOLO VOICE AND PIANO: Series III, Johannes Brahms. 64 songs, published between 1877–86, including such favorites as "Geheimnis," "Alte Liebe," and "Vergebliches Standchen." 224pp. 9 × 12.   23822-9 Pa. **$10.95**

COMPLETE SONGS FOR SOLO VOICE AND PIANO: Series IV, Johannes Brahms. 120 songs that complete the Brahms song oeuvre and sensitive arrangements of 91 folk and traditional songs. 240pp. 9 × 12.   23823-7 Pa. **$9.95**

Available from your music dealer or write for free Music Catalog to Dover Publications, Inc., Dept. MUBI, 31 East 2nd Street, Mineola, N.Y. 11501.

Dover Popular Songbooks

FIRST TIME EVER FAKE BOOK: 650 Outstanding Songs, Belwin-Mills et al. "Star Dust," "Ain't Misbehavin'," "Ol' Man River," other favorites in beautifully printed music and lyrics. 451pp. 9 × 12.
24395-8 Pa. $24.95

RICHARD WOLFE'S LEGITIMATE PROFESSIONAL FAKE BOOK: More Than 1010 Songs, Richard Wolfe. Melodies, chords, lyrics of over a century of American pop standards: Camptown Races, Amazing Grace, Over the Rainbow, Blue Moon, many more. 480pp. 9 × 12.
25019-9 Pa. $39.95

THE TOP 100 MOTOWN HITS, Columbia Pictures Publications. Piano lyrics and guitar chords for "You Are the Sunshine of My Life," "Three Times a Lady," "I Just Called to Say I Love You," "My Cherie Amour," "I Heard It through the Grapevine," and 95 more. 331pp. 9 × 12.
25017-2 Pa. $18.95

THE GREAT MUSIC OF DUKE ELLINGTON, Duke Ellington. 42 greatest songs: "Sophisticated Lady," "In a Sentimental Mood," "Satin Doll," etc. Piano, vocal, guitar chords. 20 illustrations. 143pp. 9 × 12.
20757-9 Pa. $13.95

THE STARDUST MELODIES OF HOAGY CARMICHAEL, Belwin Mills. Complete piano music and lyrics for "Lazy River," "Georgia on My Mind," "Heart and Soul," other great hits. 208pp. 9 × 12.
24682-5 Pa. $18.95

VICTOR HERBERT ALBUM: 37 Songs and Piano Pieces, 1895–1913, Victor Herbert. Tuneful treasury reprinted from rare sheet music: "Naughty Marietta," "Ah! Sweet Mystery of Life," "Toyland," "Italian Street Song," "Sweethearts," many other favorites. Introduction. 176pp. 9 × 12.
26186-7 Pa. $9.95

FAVORITE SONGS OF THE NINETIES, edited by Robert Fremont. 88 favorites: "Ta-Ra-Ra-Boom-De-Aye," "The Band Played on," "Bird in a Gilded Cage," etc. 401pp. 9 × 12.
21536-9 Pa. $13.95

POPULAR SONGS OF NINETEENTH-CENTURY AMERICA, edited by Richard Jackson. 64 most important songs: "Old Oaken Bucket," "Arkansas Traveler," "Yellow Rose of Texas," etc. 290pp. 9 × 12.
23270-0 Pa. $10.95

SONG HITS FROM THE TURN OF THE CENTURY, edited by Paul Charosh, Robert A. Fremont. 62 big hits: "Silver Heels," "My Sweetheart's the Man in the Moon," etc. 296pp. 9 × 12.
23158-5 Pa. $8.95

ALEXANDER'S RAGTIME BAND AND OTHER FAVORITE SONG HITS, 1901–1911, edited by David A. Jasen. Fifty vintage popular songs America still sings, reprinted in their entirety from the original editions. Introduction. 224pp. 9 × 12. (Available in U.S. only)
25331-7 Pa. $9.95

"PEG O' MY HEART" AND OTHER FAVORITE SONG HITS, 1912 & 1913, edited by Stanley Appelbaum. 36 songs by Berlin, Herbert, Handy and others, with complete lyrics, full piano arrangements and original sheet music covers in black and white. 176pp. 9 × 12.
25998-6 Pa. $10.95

"TAKE ME OUT TO THE BALL GAME" AND OTHER FAVORITE SONG HITS, 1906–1908, edited by Lester Levy. 23 favorite songs from the turn-of-the-century with lyrics and original sheet music covers: "Cuddle Up a Little Closer, Lovey Mine," "Harrigan," "Shine on, Harvest Moon," "School Days," other hits. 128pp. 9 × 12.
24662-0 Pa. $7.95

THE AMERICAN SONG TREASURY: 100 Favorites, edited by Theodore Raph. Complete piano arrangements, guitar chords and lyrics for 100 best-loved tunes, "Buffalo Gals," "Oh, Suzanna," "Clementine," "Camptown Races," and much more. 416pp. 8⅜ × 11.
25222-1 Pa. $12.95

"THE ST. LOUIS BLUES" AND OTHER SONG HITS OF 1914, edited by Sandy Marrone. Full vocal and piano for "By the Beautiful Sea," "Play a Simple Melody," "They Didn't Believe Me," 21 songs in all. 112pp. 9 × 12.
26383-5 Pa. $7.95

STEPHEN FOSTER SONG BOOK, Stephen Foster. 40 favorites: "Beautiful Dreamer," "Camptown Races," "Jeanie with the Light Brown Hair," "My Old Kentucky Home," etc. 224pp. 9 × 12.
23048-1 Pa. $7.95

ONE HUNDRED ENGLISH FOLKSONGS, edited by Cecil J. Sharp. Border ballads, folksongs, collected from all over Great Britain. "Lord Bateman," "Henry Martin," "The Green Wedding," many others. Piano. 235pp. 9 × 12.
23192-5 Pa. $10.95

THE CIVIL WAR SONGBOOK, edited by Richard Crawford. 37 songs: "Battle Hymn of the Republic," "Drummer Boy of Shiloh," "Dixie," 33 more. 157pp. 9 × 12.
23422-3 Pa. $7.95

SONGS OF WORK AND PROTEST, Edith Fowke, Joe Glazer. 100 important songs: "Union Maid," "Joe Hill," "We Shall Not Be Moved," many more. 210pp. 7⅞ × 10¼.
22899-1 Pa. $9.95

A RUSSIAN SONG BOOK, edited by Rose N. Rubin and Michael Stillman. 25 traditional folk songs, plus 19 popular songs by twentieth-century composers. Full piano arrangements, guitar chords. Lyrics in original Cyrillic, transliteration and English translation. With discography. 112pp. 9 × 12.
26118-2 Pa. $7.95

FAVORITE CHRISTMAS CAROLS, selected and arranged by Charles J. F. Cofone. Title, music, first verse and refrain of 34 traditional carols in handsome calligraphy; also subsequent verses and other information in type. 79pp. 8⅜ × 11.
20445-6 Pa. $3.95

Available from your music dealer or write for free Music Catalog to
Dover Publications, Inc., Dept. MUBI, 31 East 2nd Street, Mineola, N.Y. 11501.